Beyond Big Willow

by
Valerie McKinley

"For my three girls Sharon, Louise and little Elaine, whose memory we all cherish. For my late brother, Roger, my extended family and my loyal husband, Mac."

Beyond Big Willow

ISBN 978-0-9558963-1-6

Published by:
Allen Ansell T/A 'ESP' - Shoreham - BN43 6GJ - W.Sussex - UK

Edited by
Christine Ann Clatworthy

Introduction and Acknowledgements

It seemed such a self absorbed thing to do, writing a book of prose and poetry about my life. After all, who in their right mind, would want to read it? However, my eldest daughter, Sharon, who first put the idea in my head, had sown a seed in my mind which took root and refused to die. Over time I found myself, more and more, seriously contemplating the possibility. Sharon, you see, was/is always wanting to know about things long past, people long ago departed, events and happenings that, without my relating them, would vanish forever.

Then, I lost my beloved elder brother, Roger (Podge), who you will meet throughout these pages, along with my towheaded step-brother, Derek (Degs) and my elder sister, Gillian (Gilly). How could I allow the brilliantly animated images of these loved ones, who were such an intimate and important part of my life, to disappear? To become simply images on photos, with absolutely no provenance or explanation about the immeasurable richness they brought with themselves into life?

So armed with memories, impressions, some well remembered, some distant, some anecdotal, most joyful, others sad - bitter even; I began to write, and what started out as a skeletal idea intertwined with a dream, soon became an obsession.

Belonging to the writer's web site, UKAuthors, I submitted my poems and my memories, and was astounded by the positive reaction they promoted from people I had never met; their comments being mostly favourable. Someone always inspiring me to write more; many encouraging me to get them published.

I began to realise, not only was I writing about my past, but about an age and a country fast disappearing; yet there was still an interest and a nostalgia for a life-style that was all but gone, not just from members of my immediate family.

My childhood, as you will discover from these pages, was a simple one with simple pleasures, yet, when I look back, I see that I have experienced things children today can only read about or see replicated in films. I realise there was nothing dramatic in my childhood, but there were many things to be grateful for. I was lucky, for instance, to have survived TB, when only a few short years earlier, I would most certainly have died. I witnessed, along with others of my generation, things that I hope are never likely to happen again. Some horrors that never should happen again, like all out world war, capital punishment. Then there were other things that would be oh so lovely to experience again, like steam trains and working canal boats; a gentler more relaxed way of life.

Here too I would like to acknowledge that this little book would never have been possible without the love and support of my wonderful husband, Mac, whose patience with me and my moods over the months it took, knew no bounds. Also to Allen Ansell, my publisher, for his dedication and endless patience with my stupidity with all things technical. To him I owe a sincere debt of gratitude. My editor and dear friend, Christine Clatworthy, who so generously gave of her precious time and boundless energy and like Allen spoke only words of comfort and encouragement when I seemed to understand nothing.

Thanks goes too, to all my friends at UKA who have been a source of inspiration to me since I joined them in February 2004.

INDEX

'First years at Kilby Bridge'

'The Manor Street Years'

'Adult Years'

Illustrations

Plate 1

1. Gran with daughters and daughters -in- law
(back row left to right) Aunt Rose George, Aunt Nell Hewitt, Aunt Lil Greasley, Aunt Jess Hewitt , and Aunt Nelly Hewitt (front row left to right) Mum, Gran, Aunt Rose Hewitt.

2 Me and Aunt Jess Hewitt at High Kelling.

3. My Girls, Sharon and Louise.

4. Me and Aunt Jess Hewitt at Home Place, High Kelling

5.Family picnic at Kilby Bridge, in the field next to Gran's cottage (very back) step brother Dennis (next row left to right) Podge, my brother, Gilly my sister, Shirley (my step sister) Degs (my step brother) (front row left to right) My step father, Hazel, my half sister, me, Mum holding my baby half brother David.

Plate 2

1. Mum and Dad at Bradgate Park, before they were married.

2. Me and Mac getting married in 1991

3. Grandma with my baby half brother and sister. The twins, Anne and Peter

4. Granddad and Grandma at Kilby Bridge

5. Granddad paddling in the sea at Uttoft.

6. Granddad with his sons and sons- in- law.
(back row left to right) Uncle George Greasley, Uncle George Hewitt, uncle Tom Hewitt, Uncle Fred Hewitt. (back row left to right) Uncle Albert Hewitt, Granddad, Uncle Bill George

Plate 3

1. Me and Uncle George Hewitt at High Kelling

2. My wedding to David
(left to right) Father-in -Law, George Sidney, Mother-in- Law, Vera Sidney. My new husband David and me, My mum Min Swift. My brother-in-law, Alan Moore and my elder sister Gill.

3. Me and Aunt Jess Hewitt at West Runton

4. My girls Sharon and Louise

5. Me at five years old

6. Family group (left to right) Podge (Roger) Gran, Gill and me on Gran's lap.

Plate 4

1. Sharon and her father going into All Saints Church in Wigston

2. Sharon as a teenager

3. Louise and her new husband at St Peters and St James' Church Oadby after the ceremony.

4. Me at Louise's wedding

5. Mac and me about to sign the register at our wedding in 1991

Plate 5

1. Sharon and me at the Wembley International Country Music Festival in 1980.

2. Mac on the Sea Tractor at Bigbury -on- Sea in Devon on our honeymoon in 1991

3. Podge in a bar in Gibraltar during his time in the RAF

5. Mum and Dad's beautiful wedding circa 1936.

4. Podge in a bar!!

Plate 1

First Years
at
Kilby Bridge

Wednesday 26th May 1943

In the midst of conflict
with the world at war,
my father at sea,
destined to walk
his homeland no more.
I arrived,
breaking free
of the darkness
out into the light
leaving the warmth of the womb
for a cool spring night.
Not understanding then,
 for how could I see,
the man
from whose loins I sprang
would be but a shadow,
a ghost to me?

Growing up Without a Daddy

My first conscious memories are all connected to snippets of conversations spoken in whispers; phrases like: the Jerries, this bloody war, never know her daddy, poor little mite, VE day, what about the poor buggers still in Burma, when are they bringing 'em back? The Japs, The bomb, Events too stand out, like,

"Uncle Joe's coming home. He's bringing you a ginger kitten. Won't that be nice?" The fancy dress party in the Nissen hut that passed for a village hall, to welcome the men back from war. My first fresh tomato. Ugh! It made me throw up. My first banana that I wouldn't eat because it had black bits in it! Over all, the sense I was different from other kids in the village. My daddy was dead. Everyone made a fuss of me because he had never made it home to see me. I had an older sister and a big brother, but they had known Daddy and he had known them. I felt singled out, a changeling, although I couldn't have put it into words then, it was just a sense.

I used to have a recurring dream that I couldn't understand then. I would be with my family when someone would shout, "Quick! The Jerries are coming!"

A shadowy figure, who I knew instinctively to be my daddy would run to the cupboard and hide. When the Jerries came (faceless) they would go straight to the cupboard and when they opened it, Daddy had disappeared into the cupboard of our neighbour; the search would continue from house to house, until the Jerries had reached the end of the row. At the end of the row of houses, there was the canal and the bridge that spanned it; on the bridge were the words, Kilby Bridge 1936. Somehow I knew that my daddy had changed into those words and that the Jerries would never find him. There the dream ended. For years after, every time I crossed the bridge, I would run my fingers lovingly over the letters and wonder if he could feel me touching him. It's still vivid in my mind even all these years later.

Having a father who fought for his country and lost his life doing so, coloured the whole of my life; my beliefs, my politics. I cannot tolerate Fascism, I hate bigotry, I hate war. I understand the need to fight oppression for the preservation of freedom. Daddy gave his life fighting for freedom, so for me to believe differently would make a nonsense of his life and death.

My mother felt compelled to marry again so she could give us a better life. As things turned out, she regretted it often, because it made life for us much worse. My paternal grandfather disapproved of her marriage and cut us out of his will; he was a very wealthy man. Had my father lived, he would have eventually inherited a fortune. Of all of this though, I was ignorant. I grew up in a large family (my mother gave birth five times after me). We were poor but I don't blame my mother, I worshipped her. She was fun to be around and had a gift for loving and spoiling us all in her own scatty way. She was a lousy housekeeper, couldn't cook to save her life, but we all adored her. Despite having so many children, Mother was not a strong woman, having been born with a disability, and limped badly; her pain was constant but so was her optimism. She always kept her smile, her joie de vivre.

As I grew, I would fantasize about my father, what my life would have been like had he survived. He haunted my childhood constantly, until I almost went mad with a craving to see him, to know the sound of his voice; all these emotions chased round and round in my heart and mind. It was a long time before I could let go of the feeling of being cheated; yet I have never lost the conviction, one day I will meet my daddy and my hunger will finally be satisfied.

Grandpa

Grandpa looked like a fat old walrus
with his scruffy furry moustache,
chin-ward droopy, like yellowed tusks.
Gnarled hands grasp an aged spade;
booted foot poised mid air,
to dig a spit of earth for victory,
several sepia generations ago.

The photograph, creased, but still precious,
lay in my wrinkled palm,
a piece of long lost history
joyfully rediscovered in an old tin box.
Fragmented memories twinkle tentatively
through a flaky crumble of cracks
of a now disintegrated wall
of forgetfulness to dazzle and delight.

The aroma of old English humbugs,
a hairy goosegog proffered between muddy fingers
and popped into an unsuspecting mouth
to be spat out with a shudder of disgust!
A lusty laugh.

A tweaked nose, held by forefinger and thumb,
a peek-a-boo game from behind the rocking chair,
a shoulder ride to the village to buy
an accumulator for the wireless,

One last sticky kiss on
his old man's grey face,
as he lay on his deathbed
strategically placed by the parlour fire
to comfort his last earthbound hours.

Sleeping in Mummy's Bed

A shaft of light, pointing heavenward
a lone flier trapped in its beam.
A renegade relic
that haunts the hallways of my mind,
bumping now and then into a dead end
of forgotten dreams,
and bouncing forward
to stir yet another memory.
A ragged sob,
a shuddering sigh,
stifled by her pillow.

The drone of the original
and the wump, wump, wump
of a reply...
Then silence;
until the echo of weeping begins once more,
on and on to the dawn
of another sombre day,
and Mummy's red and swollen eyes.

Based on a recurring childhood nightmare. My father died from wounds received during the war when I was just 10 months old and I never knew him. That fact has always haunted me.

Kilby Bridge

I don't know how or when I became aware of the oppressive dark, or why it should make me so afraid. My infant mind sensed instinctively that my daddy was in danger, but as to the reason, I had no clue. I heard muffled voices urging him to hide in the cupboard, someone breathing hard, a shadow moving silently to obey the frightened voices.

Running, booted feet making loud stomping noises on the cobbled yard.   A clipped angry voice shouting orders in a foreign tongue, and yet I understood its meaning.

Lights flashing, men searching rooms, cupboards... Surely they would find my daddy, but no... They went from house to house, until they reached the end of the row; always, my daddy just one step ahead. Then, when they had searched all the houses, the voice shouted orders to cross the street and search there too.

It was only I who saw him; my daddy moving like a ghost onto the bridge that spanned the canal and morphing into the letters etched into the stonework of the bridge

'Kilby Bridge 1936'

As mysteriously as it had begun, the oppressive darkness disappeared along with my fear. Just my wet cheeks and hiccupping sobs remained.

I was calm now, as I felt my mother's arms around me, her sweet voice telling me daddy was safe. Nothing would hurt him ever again. And he was watching over me to keep me safe.

Each time I crossed the bridge I would touch the letters and gently run my fingers over them, wondering if he knew I was touching him, and if he was happy.

To see the Scotsman.

The pushchair
had no springs.
Every bump jarred
my baby bones.

The wheels clattered
over the gravel path.
The sound of breath,
whistling through teeth
dotted with words and whoops of delight,
made me giggle.

We headed, pell-mell,
for the bridge.
The Flying Scotsman was coming.
The brothers must see it.

I was clinging on for my life
when suddenly, clunk...
The front wheels came off!
I went flying through the air,
propelled forward - landing on my face.

My little lungs
expelled the air explosively.
On its way up, it
played a tune on my vocal chords,
pushing out a scream of agony.

Blood spurted,
tears and snot
mingled
to paint my face a horror.
Gravel in my mouth;
newly grown teeth
hung on bloody pieces of gum.

Grandma, gardening
at that precise moment,
came running.

Poor Podge and Degs
got a clip around their ear-holes
and the Scotsman flew by, unnoticed.

THE
FLYING SCOTSMAN
1862 - 1962

The Sinful Bite

Mr Griffin, the baker
wrapped the still warm loaf
in a brown paper bag.
The tantalizing yeasty aroma
of freshly baked bread
tickled and tweaked my five year old nose.

I walked away from his battered, old blue van
with an overwhelming temptation
to bite the corner from the crusty delicacy;
all fear of a stinging behind forgotten,
as the delightful smell crept further and further
up my nostrils to tease the pleasure zones of my brain.

Once bitten, chewed, savoured and swallowed
realization of the sin committed
became immense and unforgivable.

I crept through the back door,
slid the mutilated evidence of my crime
onto the kitchen table
and legged it up the stairs and into my bed,
anticipating punishment,
yet hoping to avoid the red bottom.

I fell asleep to the distant drone
of 'Dick Barton Special Agent' on the wireless;
waking, only briefly, as gentle hands
took off my dungarees and tucked me in for the night.

The Accident

Degs was sitting on the branch,
Podge had shinned half way up,
while I was at the bottom of the tree
with my dress held out
to catch the illicit plums,
all fat and juicy.

My mouth was watering
in anticipation...

"Leave them plums alone our Mu!
Keep yer eyes peeled"
Podge's harsh whisper came
hissing down the tree.

I looked guiltily around
checking this way and that.

Then I saw him,
all corduroy and gaiters.
His shot gun broken, tucked under one arm,

the other arm punching the air
his mouth moving ominously.

The plums went flying!
I was off like a rocket
toward the rally banks.

Thump, oomph!
"Wooah, watchit!"
The sound of running feet behind me.

Gasps of breath sucked into
bursting lungs...

A roar from the road;
a sickening crunch
a clatter.
Then silence...

I halted,
Podge and Degs halted,
corduroy and gaiters halted.
We all turned to gawp.

Flushed with horror
and excitement,
we headed for the road.

Plums forgotten,
eyes full of broken bodies and blood.
A mangled motor bike
a drunken telegraph pole.

A single curl of smoke
drifting from the bike,
told me time was still moving.

Abruptly, I was snatched up
in strong arms and whisked indoors.
Podge and Degs dragged by their shirt collars,
followed in sharp time, protesting loudly.

I looked back
just in time, to see two broken bodies
disappear beneath a tarpaulin...

Childhood Terror

The room was black,
heavy with the dark.
Beneath the covers
I held my breath
as fear, cold and stark,
struck me rigid;
still as death.

Floor boards creaked.
I felt a draught.
I thought I caught the sound
of the softest laugh.
Trembling, I burrowed deep
holding my blanket tight,
praying for sleep to rescue me
from the clutches
of the night.

The thump came sharp and sudden
snatching my breath away.
The lub dub of my heartbeat
quickened in the fray
of bony arms and legs
and tangled smelly feet.

Eeek! It was my older sister
prowling in the dark,
scaring me witless,
having a lark...
All of a sudden
the room flooded with light.
Mum in the doorway
dispelling the night.
A clout for my sister,
a cuddle for me,
as I looked up tearfully
saying, "I need a pee..."

Battle Scars

Something stirs;
a recollection rears before my eyes.
You in the garret, head unbowed,
 your nose bloodied from battle.

A skirmish you had won!
I would have loved to have seen your foe,
the defeated one;
your sworn enemy.
What a sight he must have been.

There were no tears,
just an ooze of blood
from your slightly swollen duke.

I had snuck up to that lofty place
where Mum had banished you
for fighting again.
My little heart hammering;
my eyes round with awe and admiration.

Later, I sneaked a slice of bread and dripping,
a rock cake and a maggoty apple, up to you.
I couldn't let the victor go hungry, could I?
After all,
there would be weightier wars to wage
on other days ...

Disobedience
The call was just too difficult to resist.

The water would call
as if it were Lorelei luring me,
yet Lorelei dwells far away,
not in the Grand Union Canal!

I would stand and sway,
dance with the reeds,
fly with the dragon fly,
lie to watch the roach;
chin cupped in grubby hands.

I became as the chameleon,
dark chestnut head amongst
a stand of bull rushes,
watching the moorhen.

Intoxicated by the salty tang
of the reeds,
hypnotized by water boatmen
skimming the surface

until the low throb - throbbing beat
of an approaching narrow boat
would snap me back,
bringing me to my bare feet.

Running to meet them
waving and calling,
"Whatcha carryin', mister?"

Then before I got an answer,
I was caught.

There on the other side,
over the wall,
my mother's angry face.
A finger pointing was enough
to send me scuttling home
with an already tingling hide,

knowing there would be
an early night
and no tea for me.

Yet I knew, next time
I would not be so impetuous.

The Fried Egg.

A memory stirs

The white of the egg,
slowly and reluctantly,
disappeared between trembling lips
and mingled with salty teardrops
lapped up by a tongue
whose buds yearned for a friendly taste.

And I just longed for my mummy
who was away buying my baby sister.

Teatime;
I stared in dismay at the lone yolk,
lying on the saucer.
Through my tears,
I could swear it winked at me.

The Rusty Nail

Would I ever understand boys??

His scream of agony brought me up from the shallow cool sparkling water of big willow as if it were a tub of boiling liquid. Something awful must have happened; he never ever made a fuss. I shook the droplets of water from my eyes and looked across the stream to the source of the commotion. He was hopping around on the bank with his right foot in the air, and protruding from it was an ugly six inch rusty nail, blood dripping over the muddy brown of the bank and onto the late spring grass, in big shiny red globs. Horse flies buzzed around in the early afternoon sunshine, excited by the prospect of a gory feast. I opened my mouth and let out a howl of fear. My brave Podge was dying from loss of blood! I fancied I could see him emptying of the life force, turning chalk white before my panic stricken eyes.

The ever increasing decibels of varying howls and screams brought the older boys scurrying across the field from where they had a game of football in progress. Heading up the posse, was Billy, my half blood cousin and secret love. His dazzling white smile soon turned to a light brown frown of concern as his intelligent eyes took in the situation. He scooped up Podge in his strong arms and started to run towards the road with blood streaming from Podge's foot, and calling over his shoulder for me to stop my howling and run on ahead to alert the gown-ups.

As soon as I arrived at Gran's cottage, I saw the aunts and uncles all there in force, guzzling tea; the air blue with cigarette smoke. A murmur of grown-up conversation was in progress, along with the serious business of the Sunday afternoon card game, as if the continuation of the world depended on it.

I tried to make myself heard above the muttering and cursing of bad luck, but I was just a baby, whining, and no one heeded my cries of distress . So, I took a great gulp of air into my tiny lungs and screamed loud enough to waken the dead! A dozen pairs of outraged eyes turned in unison in my direction and silence reigned for a beat. Gran was the first to divine that something was terribly amiss and she told Aunty Nellie, who was in the process of telling me to be quiet and stop being mardy. To "Shut up and hear what my baby has to say!" She listened intently to my hysterical rambling, then calmly instructed Uncle Tom to go down to the pub and ask the landlord, Mr Beck, to phone for an ambulance.

It became impossible after that, to keep up with events; the grown-ups all talking at once, aunts bustling around to make more tea. The only thing I knew was, I was trapped among a lot of sweaty grown-up bodies, with every one of them ignoring my pleas to be allowed to go wherever my beloved Podge was going. The time dragged after the ambulance had taken him away from me and I sat on the itchy, horse hair sofa sucking my thumb and wishing I was in heaven with my daddy; I was sure that he would put his arms around me and tell me everything was going to be all right. Degs sidled up to me with his blond hair falling over his eyes and streaks of dirt adorning his pale cheeks. He took my little hand and whispered, "He'll be alright, Mu, you see. He'll be back in no time at all!" I blinked and another tear fell off my lashes and onto my cheeks to roll with the rest of them chinwards to be gathered up by my tongue.

Presently Billy wandered over to me, picked me up and set me on his knee and started to sing 'Mr Woo' in his best George Formby voice. He made me giggle and I began to feel a little better. Gilly pushed a dish of red jelly into my hands, smiling at me. "C'mon, Mu, it's yummy," she said. I took one look at it and squawked out my revulsion. The red jelly had taken on all the

characteristics of the blood pouring from Podge's foot. I let it fall to the floor, smashing the dish to smithereens. That's when I was marched up the road to our house and right upstairs to bed and told to stay where I was until I could behave like a big girl! I must have cried myself to sleep, because the next thing I remember was Mum gently undressing me and tucking me up in my bed. "Where's Podge?" my voice, small and wobbly, demanded.
"You'll see him tomorrow, pet. He's staying at Grandma's tonight. He's fine. Nothing to worry about," she whispered, kissing me softly on the cheek.

Next morning, I ran all the way to Gran's cottage and into the parlour, to see Podge sitting in Grandpa's rocking chair with his right foot resting on a fat, goose feather cushion, bandaged up like an old man with the gout! He wore a big grin and held out the rusty nail for me to examine. " Look, Mu, ain't it a cracker? They gave it to me to keep after they took it outa me foot!" I stared at it open mouthed. Then back at Podge. Why would he want to keep the horrid thing, I thought, trying hard to puzzle out what made him so happy about it.

I watched him tie a piece of string around the head of the nail, then fasten it like a medal around his neck. " This'll be me badge of honour," he declared, proudly. "Can't go to school today Mu, so I'll beat yer at snakes and ladders instead, but don'tcha get knockin' me foot!"

Billy My Secret Childhood Love

Billy's hair is fuzzy
Billy's skin is brown
Billy's first to the top of the hill
And meets me coming down.

Billy's sister Mary
Has soft and velvet skin
With full red lips like cherries
And a wide dazzling grin.

Their daddy is a black man
From far across the sea
With his sing songy voice
He sings happy songs for me.

Billy is my cousin
Billy is my friend
When I grow up I'll marry him
Cos' he makes me laugh... The end.

The Intruder.

A true story related to me by my grandmother when I was a small girl, about how my grandfather almost killed my Aunt Annie.

Thunder rolled through the valley,
lightening split the sky;
an impatient wind tapped
at the windows and
she awoke with a soft little cry.

Ears strained,
she heard the creaking
of someone climbing the stair;
her limbs stiffened
as she listened to
hear an intruder there.

She sat up in her bed,
and swung her feet to the ground;
trembling, she awoke her slumbering man
whispering,
" Hush, don't mek a sound."

He took up his sturdy staff
waiting aback o' the door;
 aiming at his head
He'd make quite sure
the varlet would go arobbing no more.

He pulled back his hands,
staff held high.
Then, just as he was about to strike,
lightening assaulted the starless sky
and flooded the landing with light.

His daughter, ghostlike,
stood in a trance;
obeying a subconscious command.
The sleepwalking girl had narrowly missed
dying by her own father's hand.

He fell to his knees to thank the Lord
for sending that bolt of light.
Had it not been for the raging storm,
he would have been guilty
of murder that night.

Winter 1947

The yard floor was covered in sky
and reached halfway up the house.
From my bedroom window,
through mysterious lacy patterns
that had appeared there overnight,
I could see a magical place
all silent and bright.
It felt like I was the only soul
left in the whole world.
When I looked across to where the trains
chuffed and puffed past each morning,
the land lay buried and quiet
beneath, what
to my four year old eyes,
looked like fallen fluffy white clouds.

Suddenly, as if by some pre-ordained command,
all the daddies in our yard appeared with shovels
and began to make pathways in the
cotton wool clouds,
their breaths all smoky
as they chatted and laughed
and guessed that there would
be,
    "No express through today, mate.
    Looks like the cut's frozen over too, Les lad...
    No work fer me t'day then, I reckon."
My eyes moved sideways,
grew wide at what they saw.
The canal had turned all still and stiff...
The reeds and bull rushes rigid,
twinkling, as if an angel had shaken
stardust over them.

23

No school bus came
to pick up the older kids, and the yards along the terraces
grew noisy with their excited shouts
and delighted giggles.
Before long,
the strangest things began to appear.
Roly-poly white stuff men with twigs for arms,
carrots for noses, coal black eyes
and smiley pebble mouths.
Podge dressed me up in my siren suit
shoved me into my wellies,
rolled me into my scarf and tied my mittens in place
     "C'mon Mu, lets play snowballs..."
      Snowballs!
     "What's snowballs?"
     "You'll see. Don't yer get eatin' the snow neither.
     The cats 'ull 'ave peed in it!"

Barely out of the door
I discovered that the fallen sky
was wet and cold,
as a great dollop of it hit me in the chops.
My squawk of protest was heard
by all the daddies
and they turned to gawp
at the baby who was making the fuss.
     "C'mon little 'un. Snow's meant t' be fun.
     Show us what yer made of; throw one back at 'im!"
I was miserable.
After five minutes, my nose was cold and snotty,
my mouth sore, and my hands
tingled with hot aches.
So began my winter of misery...
Nineteen forty seven dragged on and on and on,
and spring seemed to belong
to another life, never to be recaptured...

The Tricycle

The tricycle tantalised me.
It stood between us
like a tyrant's taunt.
We were buddies you and I.

I lusted after the tricycle,
but it belonged to you.
I knew that you cared for me,
but you loved your tricycle more
than you prized me.

You gazed into my eyes
and saw my desire, then
laughed and peddled
away down the path
and out into the street.

"Daisy, Daisy, give me your answer do..."

That was the last time
we played together that summer.

Sulking by Big Willow

Lying on my tummy
on the bank by big willow,
using my folded arms
as a bony pillow,
I lay, sulking and angry,
planning to run away,
because Mummy had told me
I'd be going to school next day.

I smelled the earthy scent,
heard the insects buzz,
blew a dandelion clock,
inspected some mossy fuzz.
From the corner of my eye
I saw a flash of blue;
a pretty little dragonfly.
Past my head it flew!

I watched as it hovered
over big willow brook,
heard a blackbird calling,
lifted my eyes to look.
He sat far up in the willow tree,
calling to his mate and
I forgot my misery
at my future fate.

Presently, I remembered
soon I would be
another girl in school.
Not there, under the willow tree,
but sitting in a class room,
not beside this chattering brook,
staring with increasing gloom
at a stuffy exercise book.

I wanted to watch and listen,
sense the rhythms of the earth,
feel a breeze lift my hair,
grasp at life's true worth.
To run through the meadow
without shoes upon my feet,
skinny dip in Big Willow,
pick wild strawberries to eat.

Deep down inside me,
I knew it couldn't be so;
I had to learn to read and write,
I knew I had to go.
Soon I heard her calling
from across the field.
Mummy's getting anxious,
to custom I must yield.

Of course... that's not how
I viewed it then.
All those years ago,
I felt all the feelings,
all the words,
I was yet to know.

First Day

Green gloss walls,
Drab brown doors,
High cream ceilings,
Wood block floors.

Rows of little hooks
To hang small coats,
Cracked white sinks,
Scummy dirt on water floats.

The smell of sweaty feet,
Someone's eggy farts,
David Killick's snotty sneeze,
That's when the crying starts.

Please... Mummy, take me home.
School is not for me.
Take me home by Bromley's bus,
Let's go to Gran's for tea...

All my crying is for nothing,
All my tears fall in vain,
Not only does she leave me...
Tomorrow,
I do it all again !

The Bitter The Sweet

Remembering is bitter sweet.
Bitter as the very first taste of an orange,
Sweet as the wild strawberriness
of a long ago summer.
Spring,
I remember as violets
and wild garlic,
playing cuckoo under the railway bridge,
then delight
as the echo answered back.
Football games with my brothers
in the middle of the road;
never once worrying
about being knocked down
by a speeding horse and cart.
Summer,
spent fishing
for minnows and sticklebacks;
picnicking, a feast with cold tea and bread and jam.
Lazy days watching the narrow boats pass
on their way to my imagined Eldorado,
with their noisy, raggedy children and barking dogs.
Autumn
was russet reds, coppery gold,
the dry furry taste of beech nuts;
competing for them with the greedy, grey squirrels.
Fat juicy plums and stolen apples;
wood smoke mixed with the smell of rotting compost
and just harvested allotments.
Early morning mists
overlaying the canal like a gossamer blanket.
Guy Fawkes night,
with just a sparkler each
and a bonfire to bake a potato on.
The smouldering guy, finally combusting on top.
Winter
was ice on the inside of the windows,
frozen solid water in the butt.
Icicles hanging like stalactites from the gables,
glittering like crystal chandeliers

in the weak, winter sunlight.
The house smelling of rabbit stew and thyme
from dinnertime to our milky bread supper.
Candle waxed fingers going to bed;
the vapours of Vick's chest rub and a bunged up nose
and always, always not enough clothes.
With a glimmer of light at winter's heart
came Christmas,
bringing a few little gifts and some carolling.
A party of hope for a happy new year,
and an impatient yearning for a fresh green spring.

Plate 2

The
Manor Street
Years

To the Rescue

Dadaddadaaaa!
The US Cavalry had arrived
in time to rescue
the homesteaders from a fate worse than death.

Roy Rogers fired into the air
in exultation
as reinforcements crested the hills,
to swoop down and free his sweetheart
from the evil clutches of the Sioux.

The Redskins were circling,
wreaking dastardly torments
on the wretched creature bound to the totem.
Whoopin' and a hollerin' a war dance!

"Come on you lot, Mam sez we're 'avin'
our picture took!"
Gill's shrill voice penetrated,
freeze-framed the action.

Tumbleweed and cacti fractured and faded,
the totem morphed into a silver birch,
part of the copse at the top of the field,
on that English Summer Sunday afternoon.

The grainy black and white,
rag-tag family group re-emerged;
my reminiscing eyes re-focused.

I smiled fondly as
the beginnings of rebellion resonated,
then gradually crackled
into a million whispers
echoing across
the long lost decades.

Oops!

Purple pixie hood,
grey knitted mittens,
ill-fitting brown coat,
buttoned up to the neck,
almost cutting off my air supply,
red runny nose.

I sat in the barrow;
Degs holding one handle,
Podge the other.

The Wigston Gaslight and Coke,
six thirty on a winters
Saturday morning.
A rime frost coating a still dark world;
steamy breath,
frozen snot candles.
Breakfast, hours away,
bladder bursting and tummy rumbling;
my misery knew no bounds.
Rather that, than
being left behind.

"We'll tek our Mu'. She don't whine,"
Degs said.
Gilly grinned; she loved her bed
more than her brothers.

The coke fire
would be glowing, and toast made,
long before she surfaced.
My toast would taste the sweeter
for my discomforts,
my hot aches would disappear as if by magic.

If only my knickers were dry!

Smiggy and Me

Smiggy, the black and white Jack Russell,
barked excitedly; tiny paws lifting off the ground
each time his jaws snapped together.

The blackberries lay bruised and bleeding juice
 over the pavement.
My Robertson's jam-jar was smashed to smithereens,
yet the label remained intact,
and the golliwog's grin, undiminished, mocked me
from its resting place amongst the shards.

By this time, Smiggy had stopped yapping;
his pink tongue lolled between black lips.
He looked pleased with the chaos he had caused.
I stared at the bloody, gaping wound
on my knee and screamed out in agony.

Knee bathed and Elastoplasted,
I was taken to see Dr Redmond.
He, of the Johnny Walker whisky breath
and seven o'clock shadow chin.

Each bump and jolt of the Midland Red Bus
jarred my knee and squeezed out yet another
sob from my dejected little mouth,
as I felt the catgut pull
and the antiseptic sting my flesh.

A tenderly meant wipe of a scratchy hankie,
moistened with Mummy spit,
mopped up self pitying teardrops
from smudged and grubby cheeks;
a rustle of paper,
and an orange flavoured Spangle was
popped into my mouth to
lift its corners, as well as my spirits.

Slowly, light dawned. If I played my cards right,
Grandma would share her Horlicks
with me tonight.

Just Ain't Cricket!

With home-made bat
and tennis ball,
wickets chalked upon the wall,
Freddie Truman
takes his aim,
blasting the novice batsman's game.
"OWZAT!!"
screams Freddie.
"C'mon, yer out!"

"No I ain't,"
I say, with a pout.
*"It never 'it the bloomin' wicket.
C'mon, Podge. This ain't cricket!"*

Podge stares me out
with steely smile.
"LBW by a mile!"
I throw the bat onto the floor,
*"I ain't playin' with you no more
LBW! Just ain't fair.
Play with Degs you mangy cur!
I'm only a girl
but I ain't no fool!
You just made up
that stupid rule!"*

Treacle Toffee

Mum loved the wintertime.
When we were kids
she could always fool us with the clock
and get us into bed early.
While, in summertime, she re-hung
the black-out curtains.
During school holidays
she would happily let us make
treacle toffee.
Eating it, tied our tongues for hours.

The Swinging Tree

The tree stood at the top of North Junction;
our special playing place.
Someone, I never knew who,
had fixed a thick rope around a stout branch.
The rope dangled down
with a big knot tied at the end.

It was our swinging tree,
but today, there he was;
a big kid,
a stranger,
swinging from our tree.
He wouldn't let us on,
just went on swinging;
daring us, with his eyes
and a sly grin to challenge us.
There was a long silence

A stand off...

I held a knobbly stick in my hand,
not intended for a weapon;
a stick to swipe at the hedgerows
as I walked.
I held it to the ground, casual like.
The red ants began to march,
single file, along its length.

After a while, I lifted the stick
...oh so slowly and gently touched
the big kid's leg with it.
The ants seemed to like the taste
of the big kid's leg,
but the big kid howled,
jumped to the ground
dancing a macabre rhythm.

We got our swing back...

Grandmother

I stand on the patch of earth
that used to be your garden.
How surprised I am to find
myself staring down into
the smiling face of heartsease.
In its beauty, I see you.
I slip down into the past
where my life had been simple;
running your errands without
complaint, just because you asked.
I taste again, the spice
of your Sunday bread pudding
and even the castor oil
you bade me drink when I was ill.
In my imaginings,
I can picture the cottage,
you framed in the low doorway;
even smell the candle wax,
see the flickering flame,
hear the sputtering sizzle
of hot grease as it hits the
marble topped washstand by the bed.
Above all, your gentle voice
singing me to sleep at night.
I am a grandmother now;
I want to be loved as you were.
Will I be remembered
when my own grandchildren
are grandparents ? I wonder...
I catch a familiar sound
disturbing my reverie. No.
Just the echo of memory;
your gentle voice calling to me.

My Mother's Husband

He was a small, squat man
with a large bald head
that leaned permanently
to the left,
as though he always
looked askance.

He smelled of body odour,
stale smoke and
was marked by yellowed
upper lip
where nicotine
had stained his skin, as he
continually held
the ever-present cigarette
between his thin, wet lips,

When he smiled
(which was rare)
his rotten teeth
would turn the strongest
stomach sour.

Around the house
he wore a cap,
greasy flat.
In oily overalls he'd tut
and sigh
if anyone got in his way.
He never thought to say,
  "Excuse me,"
but mumbled and grumbled
through each day
and treated life like a chore.
He didn't treat my mother though;
not to a night at the pictures
or a box of Black Magic
(they were her favourites)

When she died, he cried
rather a lot.

Six months later, he had a smart new suit,
false teeth, a wig
and fancy shoes!
Then,
he took up ballroom dancing again...

Gilly

Gilly's not a wallflower
Who stands against the wall
Gilly's not a lupin
All skinny stalk and tall
Gilly's not a violet
Who shrinks beneath the bushes
Gilly's not a rose in bloom
All pink and perfume blushes
Gilly is my sister
winter, summer, spring or fall.
No matter what the season
She's the loveliest flower of all.

The Haunted Lanes of Old Wigston

He haunted the lanes
on a daily basis.
He scared us all
yet, we made fun of him,
and he knew it,
but took no notice.

His shouts announced his presence
long before we saw him,
then they would subside
to a steady hum;
Herhummm herrrhumhumm hummm.
We'd run off and hide...

His step matched the rhythm of his voice.
Poor bugger,
he really had such little choice,
but he had to get from a to b;
using the lanes it would just
be us kids he'd have to see .

While we, well, we were scared,
but so bloody cruel,
tormenting the poor man
on our way to school.
We would follow at a distance,
copying him.
When he grew silent
we would shout out,
"Come on, sing!"

He would turn, shaking his fist,
while we stood back and took the piss!

Yes, he haunted the lanes
all those years ago,
with Tourette's syndrome.
Now, I know...

These days I'm old,
I suffer a tremor.
When I hear the kids snigger
I turn cold
and remember...

Nashy Bugs and Fleas was the affectionate nickname we children gave to the National Junior School at Wigston Magna. This poem is based on a true incident. The passage of time and poetic licence may account for any inaccuracy.

Perils of the Playground

Frostbitten fingers,
chilblained toes,
fat, ruddy cheeks,
green, snotty nose.

Girls in a line,
skipping ropes whirring,
chanting rhymes
while the boys stand jeering.

Others flash past
screaming for blood,
the bully pretending
to be on the side of good.

Bold little boy
climbs onto the wall,
Harold of England
takes a fall!

An arrow let loose,
hit Harold in the eye;
we all stand and gawp
to watch him die...

Herded like sheep
back to our pens,
ashen faced teachers
take control again.

Grey light of winter
through Victorian panes,
vies with electric yellow,
our eyes take the strain.

The pins are all dropping,
yet nobody hears,
we're too busy blinking
through snot mingled tears.

Harold did not die,
he came back to class,
and now stares icily
through an eye made of glass.

The archer unknown
has always remained...
Times I have pondered,
"Was that arrow aimed?"

Norah the Nit Nurse

"The nit nurse is coming!"
the dreaded cry,
and I
would go cold with dread
for I knew my head
would be infested.

I would be sent home
with a note
and a bar of Derbac soap,
to the sound of a scoff
from the superior toff
who sat next to me
because he happened to be,
as yet, nit free.

Oh Joy!!

A tongue in cheek look back...

A shelf appeared
as if by magic,
three quarters of the way up the wall;
cornerwise.
No one could guess
what it was for,
or what it would hold
and when we asked,
we were told,
"Ask no questions
you'll be told no lies."
It came as a surprise.
We weren't expecting
anything so grand.
It was brown and
made of Bakerlite;
the screen was only nine inches,
but we could have been at the pictures.

A Bush television set!!
Bought especially to view the King's funeral.

Oh! The delight
at everything that flickered across the screen.
All done with style,
all spoken in clear, precise English.
No 'F' word,
no reality shows,
definitely no sex or violence.

The Brains Trust,
What's My Line?
Animal, Vegetable or Mineral,
Panorama and
a sanitized version of the Arabian Nights.
Cool...

Compassionate Leave

The walls rush in.
I try to make myself small.
Then, all at once
they disappear and the sun eats me up
and I am lost.

Voices call me from far away,
faces of the family parade past.
Grandma's cool hands soothe my hot temples
and they comfort me...

Refreshing liquid trickles over a fat tongue
that has plagued me
with its refusal to come down
from the roof of my mouth,
and I wonder at the sound
of rasping that tears at my labouring lungs.

A soft kiss.
A whispered, "Come on our Mu. It's time you were up!"
"Podge!" his gentle blue eyes
all teary! His shiny buttons dazzle my fevered gaze;
the blue serge of his new uniform
is rough against my cheek.
I don't care;
Podge is home, and I feel stronger already...

The TB Sanatorium At Markfield 1st Day

This is the first in a trilogy of poems about my days in the San'

I watched in shy silence
as he polished the oak block floor;
a small Italian,
an ex-prisoner of war.
He sang as he polished,
his voice loud and strong.
It was for me that he sang
his merry little song.

He wanted a smile to light up my face,
to stop me being scared of that bewildering place.
Soon, I was clapping my hands with delight.
He whispered, *"Bella Bambina, capito? You all right!"*
He gave me a wink
as he left my room,
the aroma of polish lifted my gloom.
Through the tall French windows,
the sun climbed higher in the sky.
Just for a moment, I forgot I might die.

The door flew open and in came a nurse,
hypodermic in hand; I took a turn for the worse.
"Bottoms up!" came the no nonsense voice.
I did as I was told,
there didn't seem to be a choice.
Streptomycin was pumped
into my tender little rump;
the routine became familiar,
the Italian, my friend.
The streptomycin?
Well, that saved my life in the end!

Rabbit Stew and Sister Elsie

The smell of thyme
crept up the corridor.
The sound of the dinner trolley
rolled over the polished floor;
my stomach lurched
in protest at what was in store.

Sister Elsie appeared,
tiny, ruddy and round,
yet her dainty feet
hardly make a sound.

"Rabbit stew for dinner.
Isn't that nice? Afterwards,
tapioca, or if you prefer,
you may have the rice."

"I hate rabbit stew!"
I roundly declared.
So utterly revolted, I forgot
to be scared of this pint
sized demon who ruled
by fear.
She turned aghast
at my outburst so clear.

"You'll eat up young Miss
if it takes all day.
You'll not move a muscle
till you've seen it away!"

Under my nose
the rabbit stew sat;
we stared at each other
till my stomach went, "Splat!"
Cold and congealed,
it slid down my throat,
danced around my innards;
the end seemed remote.

The emetic explosion
that came suddenly
soaked Sister Elsie
from bosom to knee.
Her face was a study -
green from the bile,
but that little battle
I won by a mile...

The stew disappeared
as fast as it came,
and never would be
on my menu again.

Summer in the San 1956

From a bed in the corner
of a small, cubicled room,
I watched summer slowly unfold.
Through tall French windows
I saw the flowers bloom
with eyes prematurely grown old.
A sward of green grass
and poplars swaying,
surveyed from a rumpled bed;
the tedious rhythm of life, set
by a time-tabled day ahead.
Ennui and impatience,
gathered apace
as each hour unhurriedly passed.
Compulsory resting,
my wretchedness amassed;
my resentment gradually cresting.
Such was the misery
of that summer of fifty six,
confined in bed-bound
isolation.
Tubercular!
God what an awful fix
for a prepubescent girl
almost in memoriam ....
Often, I'd lie anguished
on fevered nights,
imagining my life
would end prematurely;
coughing up my ragged childish lights.

A cold dark grave
could not be meant for me... surely?
When lightening stepped down
from a black velvet sky,
tearing the soft warm flesh of the night,
I thought, "What drama, if tonight, by chance, I should die?
Hang on... hang on... 'til its light.'
Months, languishing;
a rump full of Streptomycin,
breathing fresh air by the lungs full,
that summer was frustrating,
lost to me, but enticing
my impatience
to feel the sun's magic pull.
That summer's slow passage
saw my spirits return.
With autumn's fiery days I lusted for home;
at last the heat of fever
ceased to burn,
and an embryonic energy
heralded a life yet to come.

Incident on the Top Deck

He heard the click of her heels
As she skipped lightly up the stairs
To take a seat on top of the bus,
Bringing with her a whiff of 'Evening in Paris'.

The lights on the top deck were off as
The bus idled, waiting to fill at the terminus,
Well lit from the streetlights as
They gave off their soft amber glow.

He couldn't see all of her;
She sat a row back, opposite the aisle,
But he sensed she was young and pretty,
Innocently nubile.

His heart was beating a rumba,
The veins in his temples pulsed blue.
He could feel his eyes popping
And the sweat trickle into them.

His loins tingled.
He grew large against
The fabric of his trousers;
Furtively released himself
From their restriction.
Held his hard flesh with trembling hands.
His eyes slid to the side,
Head slightly tilted
To see her staring,
Open mouthed,
Not breathing
Not moving.
Caught ...like a fawn in headlamps.

Terror held her moment-
Stretching it out like forever.

For him,
Bliss, ecstasy.

Then her moment, jack-knifed... sped on.
She screamed like a wild thing,
Clattered down the stairs and
Out into the November night...

While his
Flower burst, spurted
And juddered with pleasure...

Fast forward life's loop
Action replay.

This time
His moment shrivelled and died,
As giggling derisively,
She casually rose from her seat,
Muttered "Dirty old perv!" over her shoulder
And skipped nimbly back down the stairs
To sit on the lower deck.

This is a true story. It happened in 1958, and still makes me smile.

The Gardener 1958

Golden muscled arms
glistened with sweat
in the heat of the late morning sun;
they rippled with raw strength
and made his task look effortless.

Perspiration soaked and darkened
his blonde curls,
flattening them to his handsome head.

He knew he was being watched,
of course,
and performed accordingly,
stretching and bending
his supple body, then
arms akimbo, lightly touching
snake hips,
feet planted firmly apart,
eyes staring enigmatically
off into some forbidden zone,
making him seem mysterious;
he knew he was being admired.

What a pity his brain
didn't match his magnificent body.

How funny it was to see the roller
carry on as he stopped;
how hilarious to hear his howl of pain
as it flattened his plimsolled foot.

Sonnet To My Father

Who was this man who died so long ago?
This man who fathered me in forty three,
Who showed how brave a mortal man could be.
A man I was destined never to know.
I had thought of him in so many ways,
As a small child... A handsome young man...
In ways only a fatherless girl can,
When frustration describes formative days.

My childish mind could never imagine
The face I had not seen or ever kissed,
Or the timbre of a voice never heard.
Yet I loved him; he was my flesh, my kin.
Someone I did not know, yet somehow missed
And 'Daddy' was just an unspoken word...

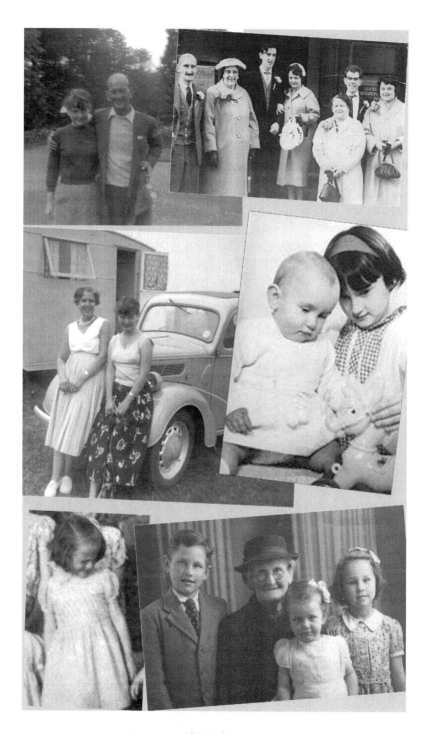

Plate 3

Adult
Years

My Sister the Cupid

My head thrown back,
mouth slightly open,
eyes shut and shoulders shaking
with convulsive laughter.

When I opened my eyes,
they were full of you
standing tall, smiling.

Confusion tumbled
through my brain.
Who were you?
Why were you standing there
looking at me that way?

My sister's voice penetrated.
"You're late. You said eight.
She has to catch the bus soon."

"Sorry, if I'd known she looked
like that I would have turned up at seven."

You didn't take your eyes off me
all the while you were talking.

I could feel the heat rising to my cheeks
and you kept looking;
those laughing, brown eyes twinkling and
flashing mischievously...

I caught the bus with the taste
of your mouth still on my lips...

Lying lips

There was no happy ever after.
You made sure of that,
with your lascivious lying lips,
 your cheating line in chat.

There was no cottage on the hill
with roses around the door;
just some frantic fondling
and lots of panting on the floor.

Just a hurried little wedding
in a back street registrars.
No romantic honeymoon
beneath the twinkling stars.

A few drinks in a sleazy pub,
all your mates gathered round;
whilst in amniotic fluid
our baby moved around.

Then, as my belly began to grow,
your ardour began to shrink;
then you began to wander
and I began to think.

What a silly girl I'd been
to believe your lying lips,
all those hot caresses
and probing finger tips...

Cause and Effect

I suspect you lurk in corners, or
somewhere on the periphery,
ready for the opportunity
to make your presence felt.
You appear at the most
inconvenient moments
calculated to catch me unawares.
Occasionally, I imagine
you take great delight
in seeing me embarrassed,
because when you pop
into my mind, I feel a blush
rise up from my toes.
You see, a thought of you
is never simple; it always comes
with a large side-order of erotica
and I am terrified people
can see me tremble at the effect,
for I am convinced they know the cause.

A Special Place in Time

A moment in time;
a happy place,
so special,
whenever
my life grows dark
I escape there.

It is filled with light,
life and vigour
with no despair.

A new beginning;
the beginning
of your life,
my little one fair.

The indescribable joy
your being
brought me
is immeasurable,
beyond compare.

It enriched my life.

I remember
the moment your little body
freed itself from mine.
That moment was illuminated,
forever marking the moment,
making it fine...

The most precious place
in time and space
in all of my existence.

Careless Moment 1961

(Confession to my daughter, Sharon)

The summer was sunny and hot that year,
 you were just a tiny tot, my dear.
It was Friday, the butcher had called.
You decided to explore, so away you crawled.

I stood on the front step, chatting away,
then remembered where I'd left you to play.
I made my excuses and closed the front door,
hurried to the kitchen finding an empty floor.

The back door stood open; you were gone.
With my heart in my mouth the hunt was on.
You were nowhere in sight. The gate stood ajar;
I imagined your small body crushed under a car.

Oh, dear God, forgive me for being so slack.
I'll do anything on earth if I could just get you back.
I flew up the entry, out into the street,
the devil at my heels, wings on my feet.

I looked up and down, you were nowhere to be seen,
my whole world turned as dark as it ever had been.
Perhaps she's next door, I suddenly thought,
so back down the entry I ran, all distraught.

As I turned into the gate to go next door,
I suddenly caught sight of you on the coal house floor;
you were chuckling, happy, having a whale of a time,
your mouth full of coal, covered in grime.

I stood there staring, crying with shame,
whilst over and over, I uttered your name.
I vowed, then and there, not to let you from my sight,
as the sound of your laughter made my whole world
come right.

Summer Cheat

A slow realization of self worth.

Inconstant heart, deceitful soul,
I remember you.
You drank my blood,
swallowed me whole.
What was I to do?

You fed my dreams with delicious plans.
I greedily lapped them up,
filling our summer nights
with love so grand,
draining my emotional cup.

You sucked me dry of feeling,
I hurt so much inside,
my broken heart reeling,
all dignity had died.

I tried so hard to mend our love,
but you did not want to know;
tossed aside like an empty glove,
I had nowhere to go.

The rest of that loveless year
I survived from day to day,
then suddenly, the spring was here
so I sloughed my blues away.
I opened wide my eyes to see
how beautiful
my life was.
I was worth so much more to me.

Why?

Because ... because ... because.

Louise

Louise, growing up
A carefree child;
Loving and giving
But slightly wild.

She tormented her sister,
Drove us all mad
With her constant questions.
What energy she had!

The noise she made
Was enough for two.
How to go quietly
She hadn't a clue.

There was only one time
She wasn't shouting or leaping,
That was the time
Our little darling was sleeping.

Flibbertigibbet
Will-o'-the-wisp
Had nothing at all
On our little Miss.

She chatted or gossiped
Her way through the day;
Her one aim in life,
Uninhibited play.

Now she's a woman
With children of her own
Sympathy, at last,
For her old mum she's shown!

Louise fully grown
Is a beautiful mother

But, sometimes... just sometimes
There are shades of that other!!

The Image of You

For Elaine

The last time
I saw you
they were
taking you away;
someone
whispered gently,
"You will see her later today."

Sleep now,
you really need to rest;
your babies need warmth.
You know it is for the best.

After some hours,
your tiny sister
was brought to my side;
in that very instant
I knew
that you had died.

You fought bravely,
at least,
they told me so.
They would not let me see you,
so, how could I ever know?

During that
fleeting moment,
before they took you
away from me,
I saw you struggle to take a breath;
such a haunting scene.

64

That single image
stayed with me ever since.

Your identical twin sister though,
has managed to convince
that, had you lived,
another image
I would see.
One just as lovely
and beautiful as she.

Daughters of Necessity

I knew I could never go back there,
life's tapestry is The Fates' business.
If they had elected to tie a bloody
great knot on the cusp of my seventeenth year,
how could I, a daft adolescent mortal,
unravel it?
Even if I had managed to,
who's to say I would have chosen
the right thread Koltho spins to cling to?
No, it's far too late for regret.
What happened, happened.
Look forward; better to forget.
Lakhesis's threads lengthen.
Try not to waste the rest of the weave.
Best foot forward, try to believe
before Atropos makes her final cut,
the whole picture will make sense
when put to the test.
The knot became a bud
that continues to bloom and grow
across the fabric of my life,
becoming a rose
with offshoots of its own.
Even if it were possible,
I would feel no desire to return to unpick it.

Grandma's Passing.

We were the last to see
that ancient yellowing flesh
still tepid, barely alive.

Me and Uncle George.

She knew
someone was there
but not who.

Each time we moved,
her open mouth
would follow the movement;

like a fledgling sparrow,
all beak and no feathers,
waiting to devour the worm.

By nine the next morning
the worm had devoured her.

Mother of the Bride (Sharon's Wedding)

Haute Couture

She wore a hat of coral pink feathers,
layered amongst copious chestnut curls.
One large feather clung, irresistibly,
along her cheek.
A cream dress of rich raw silk
draped a curvaceous body;
tiny feet encased by the softest calf skin,
high heeled and strappy,
the colour of the hat feathers.

(In her minds eye) Parisian chic;
a woman with style,
cast in haute couture,
her ensemble worn with pride,

(In reality) her role, discreet.
She was just the mother of the bride.

A Grand Night Out

It was to be a grand night out
with music and dancing.
He had refused to dance,
said he would rather watch
so they sat together in silence.
She heard the merriment of their friends;
envied them.
He excused himself, went off to the men's room.
She used to say he had the fastest zip in the west
because he always came back
before she was aware he had gone.

That night was different;
he was gone for an age.
The dancers
whirled and twirled,
twirled and whirled,
whilst she sat alone waiting,
and the knot of fear in her belly grew
with each passing second.
She took herself off
and found him
in the arms of her best friend,
laughing down into her eyes;
his mouth just above hers,
their breaths mingling,
hips touching,
swaying in time to the music.
She felt invisible,
as though she had ceased to exist;
of course, in a way she had...

Night Out

Thumb and forefinger
caress my arm,
tingling pleasantly at first,

A whispered, " What would you like to drink?"
"Just a slim-ine tonic, please," I answer.

Thumb and forefinger
become a vice,
nipping at my flesh in a bruising pinch,
bringing tears to my eyes.

"Bitch, bloody sanctimonious bitch!
Trust you to spoil a good night out."

The drink is slammed down in front of me.
The scent of juniper rises;
the look on his face dares me to argue.

"I don't... "

My spirit is as bruised as my flesh.
Words of protest freeze on my lips;
unshed tears clog my throat.

A treacherously comic dewdrop
hangs from my nose. I dash it away, angrily,

from the other side of the table comes
a triumphant laugh...

The Last Waltz

Adrenaline raced,
screamed through each highway of blood
until it slammed into her heart,
piercing her very soul,
as she watched,unwillingly,
the tableau before her.

They stood so close...

So close that
she could not tell
where the woman had began
and the man ended.

Her world tilted,
fragmented, shattered
into a zillion pieces of nonsense.

The sob rose from deep within,
accompanied by Englebert Humperdink
announcing, melodiously, that
the last waltz
had begun...

Bitter Sweet in January

As Janus looked back, as well as forward,
so January became for me.
At the crossroads of my life
I looked back
and knew I must be free.

My fight would be sad, painfully long,
frighteningly hard to bear.
I thought of giving up;
continuing
to go on suffering there.

The face I showed the world
wore contentment,
but, deep inside, I was raw;
my private face was etched with living hell;
a face no-one ever saw.

So January saw my rebellion...
Almost a life-time had gone.
I rejected his jealous ranting, rages;
escaped,
ran away.
Hurried on.

Two years passed alone;
carefree,
content.
Then I met you...
my destiny,
on that other magic, January day
irrevocable ...
Don't you see?

You became my way forward,
my future.
You transformed me,
made my true face appear;
smiling,
radiant,
all because of you,
my beloved one
so dear...

Our Mulberry Love

We found each other in our mulberry days
When the blood was meant to be cool and sane.
We laughed and talked... grew breathless;
then recognition became ... oh... so plain.
Conversation halted... Our eyes met... Held... We knew
We had been given something special, granted only to the few.
Love had come to visit a second time.
Life offered us another chance;
Another bite of the sweet, red cherry,
Another tango in the universal dance.
This time the dance won't end till both of us are done;
Dancing into death and eternity,
forever, on and on and on...

Fulfilled

A Cinquain

I came
To you trusting.
Wanting your softest touch,
Needing your love, being fulfilled
I came.

Straying Footsteps

Our journey began long ago
when we were both such children.
Yet, I remember thinking it would last forever;
thought it would end when we ended.
At first, I hadn't cared to look back.
It didn't occur to me to check
we were headed in the right direction;
I was happy to skip on, regardless.
I assumed we would get there in one piece,
together of one heart, one mind.
I really don't remember when or why
I felt the urge to turn and look back at our footsteps.
How shocking to find that yours had veered away,
straying far from mine; the gap ever widening.
I tried so hard to lure you back
to the pathway we had shared for so long.
You made it clear you were tired of my route;
I could see your tread had become lighter.
You no longer wanted to carry the burdens
we had acquired. You preferred to go on alone.
Unaccompanied you were too, right to the end
of the road you had chosen to follow.
How lonely that last mile must have been;
how desolate those last few paces.
My journey continues
with a new travelling companion.
This time I keep looking back at the footprints
to see if we are still in step (we are).

Restlessness

The tip of your finger
tickles my upturned palm;
I wake; a momentary amnesiac.

The morning stamps
through my head,
kicking my brain into remembrance.

Your features fall into place;
a groan escapes my mouth
before I can restrain it.

I stretch my lips into
a caricature of a smile
and mime, "Good morning,"

dropping my eyelids
over my disillusionment
before you even notice it's there.

I love you. You feel secure.
So you should be...
It's not your fault, I need more.

Awaking

Some mornings
When I awake, I think
It is you who lies beside me.

My heart lurches
At the thought.

Just as I shake off the last
Vestige of sleep,
I feel you.

Then reality dawns
And I remember you are dead.

Your essence fades
As though you had never existed.

I find myself wishing you back.
Then, there is a stirring
From the other side of the bed

And I think, "What is this treachery?"

A Reflection

What is time?
The word, whispered on a sigh
dampens my surface
with misty breath.
The images that come and go
register little with me, yet
to those who peer into my depths
this noun, 'time'
teases and taunts.
A smile, a frown, a blush, and tears.
I reflect them all
as their years pass,
while I,
the glass, stay placid.
Their panic rises to haunt with age;
they come to despise me
with a rage
I do not understand.

The Last Time.

Gaunt was always
the word that fitted you best.
Even from the first time I saw you

it suited you;
added a mysterious air
to your 'devil may care'
demeanour.

Tall and slim
to the point of scrag-end, I used to joke;

that was when
we were still in love,
could still laugh at each other's silliness.

Gaunt, was still
how I saw you that last time.

By then you were
staring from liver diseased eyes,
grinning with cigarette stained teeth,

smelling of decay and cheap whiskey.
There was no longer any mystery
yet, the devil remained...

Uncaring.

The Way They Were

The glory days
are embossed on my inner eye.
Intense, dazzling, like the sun's imprint
on the corporeal eye
when staring at it without protection.

It's always there
nudging my mind into remembrance.
Two little girls;
one, chestnut haired, one, golden.
One tall, one small; yet sisters.
Laughing and loving,
tears, fears.
Yet always loyal and trusting.

So many years have passed;
gone forever.
Except for their shadows,
dancing on the screen of reminiscence.

Sisters still.
Precious times,
alive only within my heart.
So much clutter between them.
So many lonely miles apart.

The Tear

I remembered something tonight;
something she told me
after you'd passed away.
It didn't signify then,
yet tonight,
it seems important somehow.
She said,
as you breathed out
your last seconds of life,
a tear trickled down your hollow cheek.
It occurs to me now,
I wish I knew who
that tear had been shed for.
The children?
All those wasted years?
Could it have been for me?
Yourself?
If only I had been there at the end
to hold your hand.
If only I had been stronger,
if only.
If...

Overload

Mybrainoverflowswithwords
in no particular order.
Theyspillfrommymind
hit the floor with a thump.
Myheadspinsoutofcontrol
and I fall with the words.
Mythoughtsburnuplifemiles
yet I stand stock still
Whiletheworldwhirlsaroundme.
I want to capture the words
buttheyflashpasttoofasttocatch.
Then, I forget which of them I want to save.

After decades of feelings of unresolved guilt at never holding my late daughter, Elaine, never being able to kiss her or tell her that I loved her, I was finally helped by a good friend, to track down her resting place. The following poem was the result of the long awaited visit to her graveside.

The Grave of Lost Babes

The air hung humid,
the sky overcast,
traffic droned on and on,
birds fluttered between
old, serried headstones.

The sun slipped out between clouds,
lit a patch of grass, freshly mown.
Its pungent aroma added, somehow,
to the sense of raw emotion
rising from somewhere deep
inside my subconscious self.

For forty-two years it had lain;
trampled down by the strictures
imposed by ignorance and arrogance.

Leaves rustled in the slight breeze
that sprang from nowhere in particular.
Inside, something loosened;
the dam burst and the years of
hurt and guilt rose
like bile in my throat.

Why had I not screamed at them?
'She is mine!'
I should have fought to hold her in my arms;
no one had the right to take her from me,

Why did I let them put her in an anonymous
grave?
A grave of lost babes...

Here, at last,
her resting place;
a good place.
My anger and guilt subsided,
my grief remained. For a while
to be replaced by great peace.

Yes. This is a beautiful place.

Faded Collection

When I was a child,
I collected spiders webs
from the hedgerows in a forked stick;
dripping morning dew, sparkling
like diamonds in the sunlight.

As I grew into a teenager
I slept in my room cocooned
by walls filled with Elvis' eyes
adoring me.

As a young mother,
I would hoard
the smiles and sticky kisses
of my children with pride.

Later, in middle age,
love became rare and elusive,
difficult to hold on to.
Harsh words and heartache
were collected all too easily.

Now in old age I catch
faded memories in a cleft stick
and blow away the dust
from the cobwebs
to see more clearly
the collected storms and teacups,
and I smile wistfully at life's irony.

Kith and Kin

Last night, I dreamed I was a child again,
with friends, siblings; playful and full of fun.
Last night I ran free; supple, without pain.
Laughing, breathless in the heat of the sun,
feeling its rays warm on my upturned face.
Squealing in rare delight at being young;
chasing companions through the open space
of forbidden fields where corn shoots had sprung.

Last night was just a dream of bygone days
that cannot return in reality;
kith and kin have gone their separate ways;
aged now, but still I love them mightily.
Our old bones complain, but our glad hearts sing
with golden memories that yesterdays bring.

Spring of Hope

A world awash with war,
I drifted in with scent of death
and springtime showers
that lingered.
Life support rationed
and formed into
queues of necessity.

A lifetime later,
the smell trickles back
tinged with apathy.

No queues.
Full bellies.

Half a world away,
hunger and horror strike,
but our telly-sotted minds
are immune.
Sometimes it intrudes;
we send money to salve our
intermittent consciences,
then continue our safe lives.

Shaken by a terrorist bomb,
we take fright,
freeze for a beat,
worry...
But further media frenzy
focuses on the latest
celebrity scandal.
Curiosity juices flow.
We lap up each drop greedily;
not able or ready to distinguish between
the stink of corruption
and the sickly smell of war.

How I yearn for a fragrant springtime,
tender, green shoots of hope.
The stench removed
forever.

Plate 4

Plate 5